Beyond Strange Street

written by Kaye Umansky
illustrated by Steve Smallman

Chapter One

The Wild Woods

Sam lay in bed with her fingers in her ears. How could she sleep, with all that noise coming from the room next door? The television was turned up, but she could still hear loud, cross voices.

With a sigh, she got out of bed. She put on her slippers and her dressing gown. Then, very quietly, she opened the bedroom door, crept past the living room and let herself out of the flat.

The empty lift stood across the landing. The doors were open.
"Time to visit Strange Street, I think," said Sam. "I wonder what it will be like this time?" And she stepped inside.

The magic button was there. One push, and she would be in Strange Street again. The best thing about Strange Street was that it changed every time.

She looked closer at the button.

The letters had changed.

They now read W. W.
How odd!
"Oh well," thought
Sam. "Here goes!"

She pressed the button.
Up went the lift
with a ...

The doors opened. Sam got a shock. Where was Strange Street? It was nowhere to be seen. Instead, there was a little track winding away between tall trees. A sign was nailed to a trunk. It read:

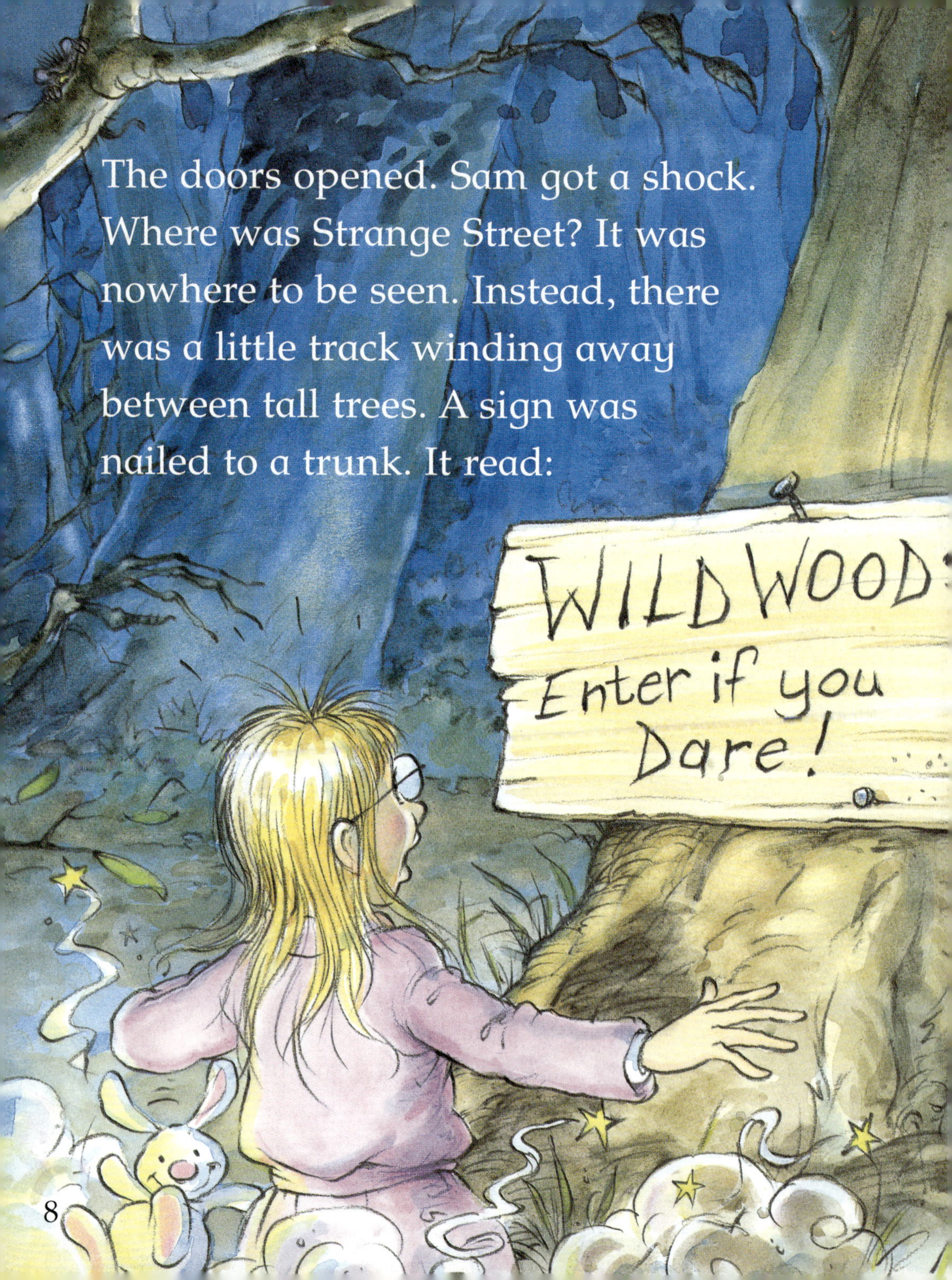

"W. W." said Sam. "Wild Woods."
Feeling excited, but just a bit scared,
she set off along the moonlit path.

Chapter Two

Obby

Sam walked on and on. The track twisted and turned this way and that. There were small, scuttling noises.

Once, a rabbit hopped across the path.

An owl hooted and
made her jump.
Sam was cold and
lonely.
She wondered if
she should go back.
And then ...

Sitting on a log by the side of the track, was the strangest little creature she had ever seen. It was covered in tufty hair. Two big ears stuck out on each side of its head. Two small eyes peered from a round, flat face. On top of its head was a huge pair of glasses. In one paw was a basket full of red spotted toadstools.

"Don't just stand there staring, silly big girl!" snapped the little creature. "Help me look!" It jumped up and began kicking angrily at the leaves.

"Look for what?" asked Sam.

"My glasses, of course! I put them down somewhere. But where? I'm bothered if I know."

"Try the top of your head!" said Sam, pointing.

"Really?" The little creature reached up and felt for them. He had such a funny look on his face that Sam had to giggle.

"Think I'm rude? Calling you silly?" he asked, hooking the glasses over his ears.
"Well …" murmured Sam.
"Well, I am. That's because I'm an Obbygobulum."

“A what?” said Sam.

“An Obbygobulum. We’re known for being rude and grumpy. But there’s one good thing about us. We always return favours. Name?”

“Sam,” said Sam.

“Obby,” said the Obbygobulum and stuck out his paw. It felt warm and furry.

"I've never heard of an Ob– obgob ..." began Sam.

"Obbygobulum. Not from round here, then?"

"No. I came in the lift."

"Ah. Pressed the magic button, eh?"

"Yes. I thought I was going to Strange Street."

"Oh, you're **way** beyond Strange Street. You're in the Wild Woods now."

"I know," said Sam, with a shiver.

"Cold?" asked Obby.

"Freezing," Sam admitted.

"Want to come back to my cave?"

He pointed into the trees. "Not far. Over by the bog. I'll make you some hot toadstool soup."

Cave?

Bog?

Toadstool soup?

"No thanks, Obby," said Sam. "I must go home now."

“But I’ve got to pay
back the favour!”
shouted Obby,
stamping his foot.
“Got to! It’s the
Obbygobulum way!”

“But it’s late,” said Sam. “It’s a long way back to the lift.”

A sudden grin appeared on Obby’s face. “Ah,” he said. “Now, there I can help you!”

He clapped his paws.

There was flash of green light. A nearby tree trunk split open with a crack!

Inside was the lift!

"How did you do that?" gasped Sam.
"That's nothing," said Obby.
"We Obbygobulums can do lots of clever things. You'll see when you come again. You will come again, won't you?"
"Of course," said Sam.
"I'll bring my friends."

She stepped in. The doors closed.

"That was the wildest adventure yet," thought Sam.